PIANO VOCAL GUITAR

KINGS OF LEON

COME AROUND SUNDOWN

ISBN 978-1-61780-413-7

HAL•LEONARD®
CORPORATION
7777 W. BLUEMOUND RD. P.O. BOX 13819 MILWAUKEE, WI 53213

In Australia Contact:
Hal Leonard Australia Pty. Ltd.
4 Lentara Court
Cheltenham, Victoria, 3192 Australia
Email: ausadmin@halleonard.com.au

Visit Hal Leonard Online at
www.halleonard.com

CONTENTS

THE END

Words and Music by JARED FOLLOWILL,
MATTHEW FOLLOWILL, NATHAN FOLLOWILL
and CALEB FOLLOWILL

Moderately fast

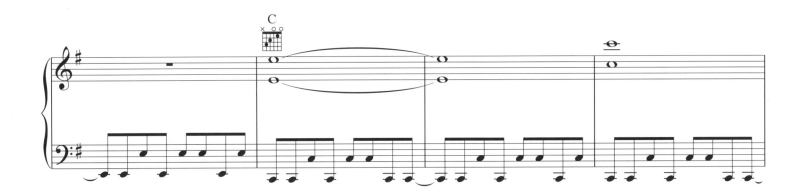

* Recorded a half step lower.

RADIOACTIVE

Words and Music by JARED FOLLOWILL,
MATTHEW FOLLOWILL, NATHAN FOLLOWILL
and CALEB FOLLOWILL

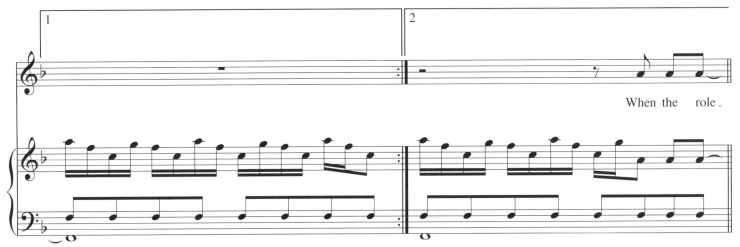

PYRO

Words and Music by JARED FOLLOWILL,
MATTHEW FOLLOWILL, NATHAN FOLLOWILL
and CALEB FOLLOWILL

MARY

Words and Music by JARED FOLLOWILL,
MATTHEW FOLLOWILL, NATHAN FOLLOWILL
and CALEB FOLLOWILL

THE FACE

Words and Music by JARED FOLLOWILL,
MATTHEW FOLLOWILL, NATHAN FOLLOWILL
and CALEB FOLLOWILL

Moderately

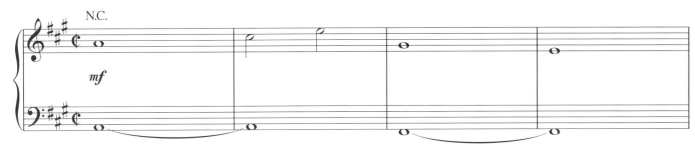

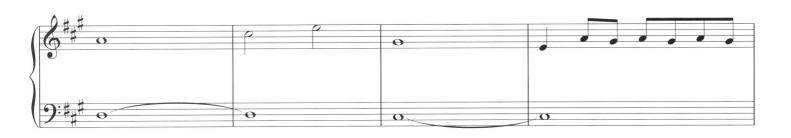

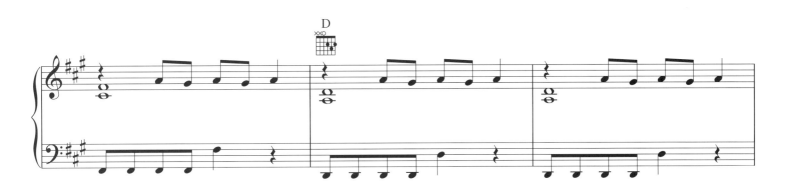

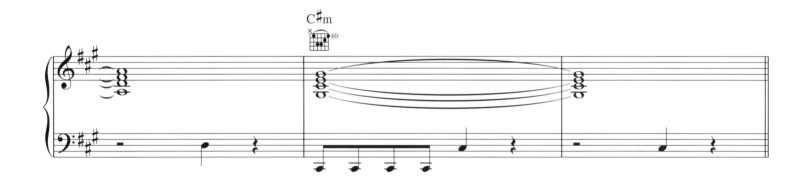

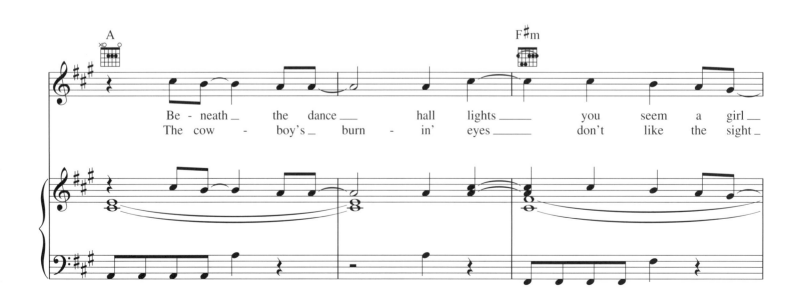

Be - neath __ the dance __ hall lights _____ you seem a girl
The cow - boy's __ burn - in' eyes _____ don't like the sight __

THE IMMORTALS

Words and Music by JARED FOLLOWILL,
MATTHEW FOLLOWILL, NATHAN FOLLOWILL
and CALEB FOLLOWILL

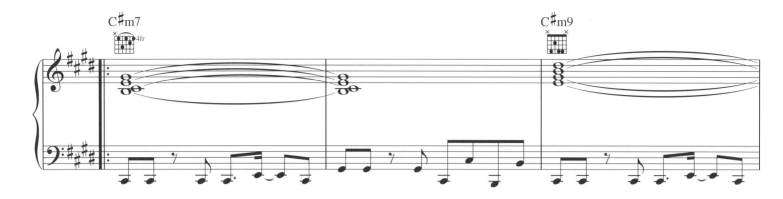

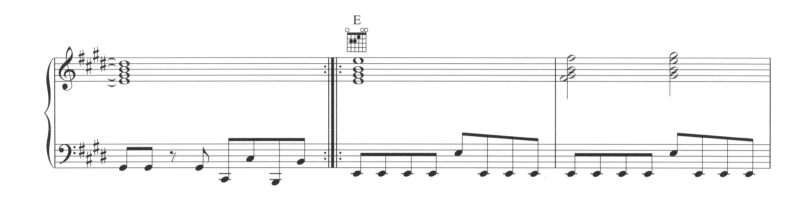

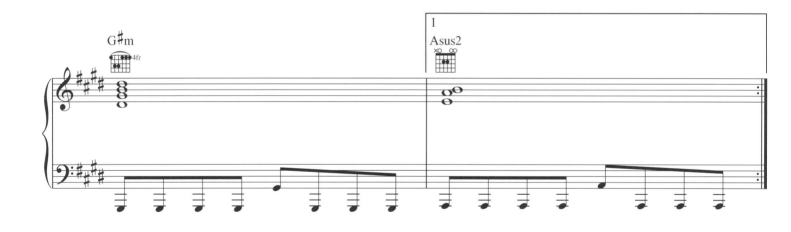

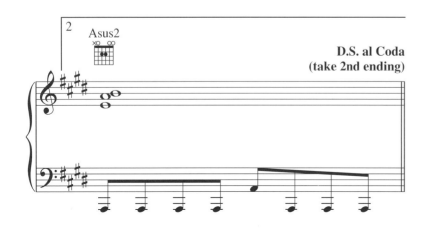

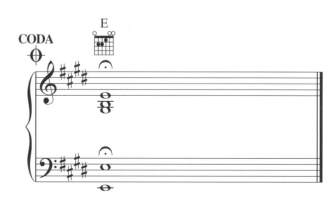

BACK DOWN SOUTH

Words and Music by JARED FOLLOWILL,
MATTHEW FOLLOWILL, NATHAN FOLLOWILL
and CALEB FOLLOWILL

Moderately

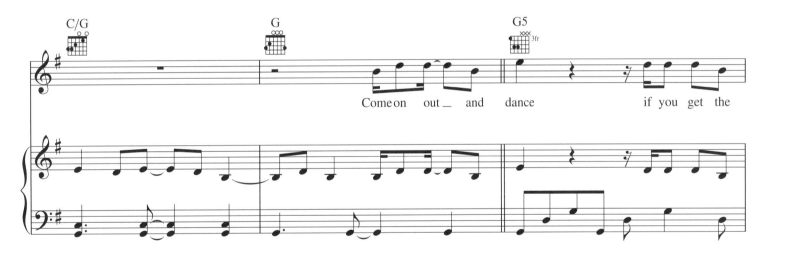

Come on out __ and dance if you get the

chance. We're gon - na spit on the ri - vals. All I want __ to know __

BEACH SIDE

Words and Music by JARED FOLLOWILL,
MATTHEW FOLLOWILL, NATHAN FOLLOWILL
and CALEB FOLLOWILL

Moderately fast

Got an at - ti - tude,
big _____ thing,

think - in' that it's al - ways right.
ev - 'ry-thing your heart de - sires.

NO MONEY

Words and Music by JARED FOLLOWILL,
MATTHEW FOLLOWILL, NATHAN FOLLOWILL
and CALEB FOLLOWILL

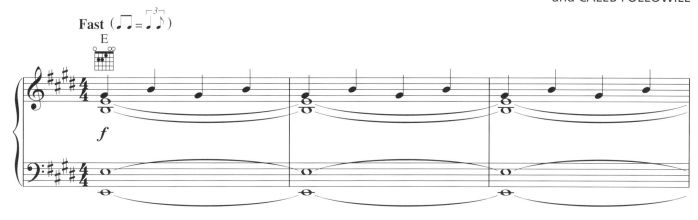

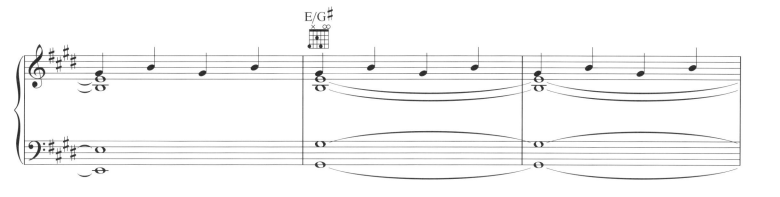

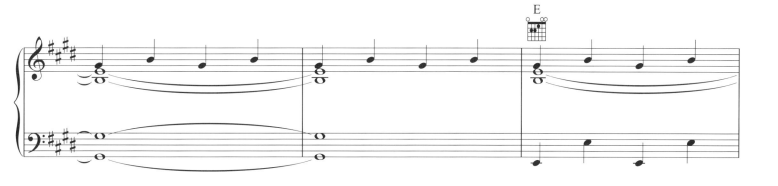

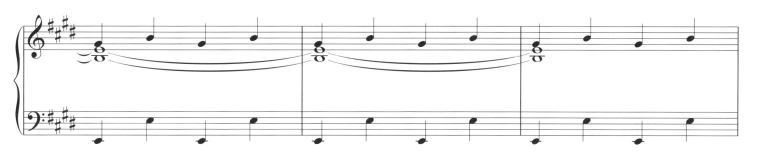

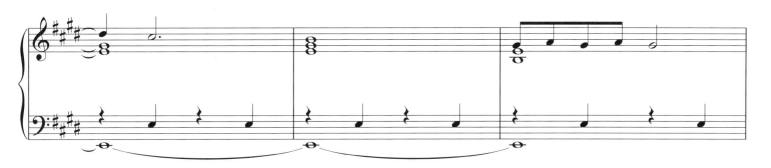

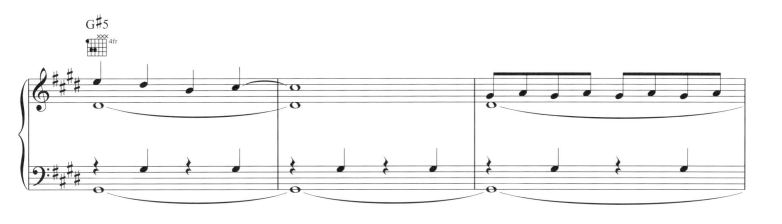

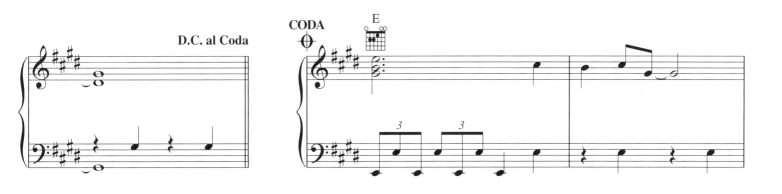

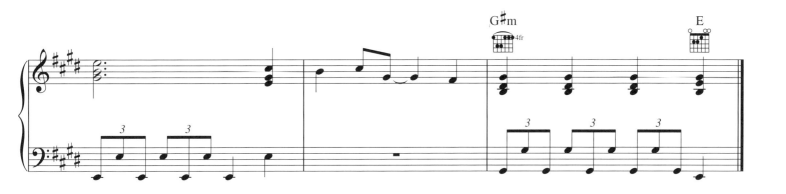

PONY UP

Words and Music by JARED FOLLOWILL,
MATTHEW FOLLOWILL, NATHAN FOLLOWILL
and CALEB FOLLOWILL

I got a ra-zor sharp __ mind that wants to cut __
Oh, if you take my hand, __ I'm gon-na get you

BIRTHDAY

Words and Music by JARED FOLLOWILL,
MATTHEW FOLLOWILL, NATHAN FOLLOWILL
and CALEB FOLLOWILL

It's in the way ___ she al-ways calls me out. ___
Walk in' her home ___ with a grass-y feel. ___

It's in the cut ___
Fall - in' and laugh -

___ of your pret - ty gown.
in' at the drinks we spill.

you.

D.S. al Coda

you.

MI AMIGO

Words and Music by JARED FOLLOWILL,
MATTHEW FOLLOWILL, NATHAN FOLLOWILL
and CALEB FOLLOWILL

PICKUP TRUCK

Words and Music by JARED FOLLOWILL,
MATTHEW FOLLOWILL, NATHAN FOLLOWILL
and CALEB FOLLOWILL

just so you know.